ONE
QUESTION A
DAY FOR US

DAILY REFLECTIONS
FOR COUPLES

Answer the question on each page with someone special and see how your responses change over the years!

Simply write the year in the space provided and then pick a bird each to jot down your answer next to. See how your answers change as time passes and you grow together.

January 1

What is your ideal way to spend a vacation?

Year:

Year:

Year:

January 2

What makes you like a person?

Year: _____

Year: _____

Year: _____

January 3

Do you think you are confident? Why or why not?

Year:

Year:

Year:

January 4

What about yourself are you most proud of?

Year: _____

Year: _____

Year: _____

January 5

What would the best version of you be like?

Year:

Year:

Year:

January 6

What life experiences did you miss out on?

Year: _____

Year: _____

Year: _____

January 7

When are you the most "you"?

Year: _____

_____

Year: _____

_____

Year: _____

_____

January 8

How did you fall out with someone close to you?

Year: _____

_____
_____
_____
_____
_____

Year: _____

_____
_____
_____
_____
_____

Year: _____

_____
_____
_____
_____
_____

January 9

Are you happy with the people
you surround yourself with?

Year:

Year:

Year:

January 10

What musical instrument do you wish you could play?

Year: _____

_____
_____
_____
_____
_____

Year: _____

_____
_____
_____
_____
_____

Year: _____

_____
_____
_____
_____
_____

January 11

What event has changed the course of your life?

Year:

Year:

Year:

January 12

What is the nicest compliment you have received?

Year: _____

Year: _____

Year: _____

January 13

What age would you like to live to, and why?

Year: _____

_____

_____

_____

_____

_____

_____

Year: _____

_____

_____

_____

_____

_____

_____

Year: _____

_____

_____

_____

_____

_____

January 14

If you could travel to any country in the world
for one month, where would you go and why?

Year: _____

_____

_____

_____

_____

_____

_____

Year: _____

_____

_____

_____

_____

_____

_____

Year: _____

_____

_____

_____

_____

_____

January 15

What is your favorite memory of someone who is not in your life anymore?

Year:

Year:

Year:

January 16

How superstitious are you?

Year: _____

_____

_____

Year: _____

_____

_____

Year: _____

_____

_____

January 17

What has been a recurring theme in your life?

Year: _____

_____

_____

_____

_____

_____

Year: _____

_____

_____

_____

_____

_____

Year: _____

_____

_____

_____

_____

January 18

What do you think happens after death?

Year: _____

Year: _____

Year: _____

January 19

What are your top 5 rules for life?

Year:

Year:

Year:

January 20

What is your favorite thing in your / our house?

Year: _____

_____

_____

_____

Year: _____

_____

_____

_____

Year: _____

_____

_____

_____

January 21

What book or movie do you wish you could experience for the first time again?

Year: _____

Year: _____

Year: _____

January 22

What petty thing that people do really gets on your nerves?

Year: _____

_____
_____
_____

Year: _____

_____
_____
_____

Year: _____

_____
_____
_____

January 23

What brings meaning to your life?

Year:

Year:

Year:

January 24

What is something you wish you could say to people but can't?

Year: _____

_____
_____
_____

_____
_____
_____

Year: _____

_____
_____
_____

_____
_____
_____

Year: _____

_____
_____
_____

_____
_____
_____

January 25

What are some of the most attractive traits a person can have?

Year:

Year:

Year:

January 26

What is a secret you have never told anyone?

Year: _____

_____

_____

_____

_____

Year: _____

_____

_____

_____

_____

Year: _____

_____

_____

_____

_____

January 27

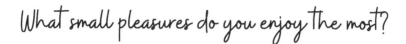

What small pleasures do you enjoy the most?

Year:

Year:

Year:

January 28

Who is the most interesting person you know?

Year:

Year:

Year:

January 29

What has been your biggest mess up so far?

Year:

Year:

Year:

January 30

What have you struggled with your entire life?

Year: _____

_____

_____

_____

_____

Year: _____

_____

_____

_____

_____

Year: _____

_____

_____

_____

_____

January 31

What is the most significant change you
would like to make in your life?

Year:

Year:

Year:

February 1

What do you want out of life?

Year: _____

_____
_____
_____

_____

Year: _____

_____
_____

_____

Year: _____

_____
_____

_____

February 2

What calms you down the most?

Year:

Year:

Year:

February 3

What kind of things do you find repulsive?

Year: _____

_____
_____
_____
_____
_____
_____

Year: _____

_____
_____
_____
_____
_____
_____

Year: _____

_____
_____
_____
_____
_____
_____

February 4

What would your perfect life look like?

Year:

Year:

Year:

February 5

If you received a salary to follow whatever passion
you wanted to, what would you do?

Year:

Year:

Year:

February 6

What is your most embarrassing
story about being sick?

Year:

Year:

Year:

February 7

What friend have you not thought
about in a long time?

Year: _____

_____

_____

_____

_____

_____

Year: _____

_____

_____

_____

_____

_____

Year: _____

_____

_____

_____

_____

_____

February 8

What's the craziest thing that happened at work?

Year:

Year:

Year:

February 9

Who do you act nice around but secretly dislike?

Year: _____

_____

_____

_____

_____

_____

Year: _____

_____

_____

_____

_____

_____

Year: _____

_____

_____

_____

_____

_____

February 10

If money was no object, how would you decorate your / our house?

Year:

Year:

Year:

February 11

How good are you at reading people?

Year: _____

_____

_____

_____

_____

_____

Year: _____

_____

_____

_____

_____

_____

Year: _____

_____

_____

_____

_____

_____

February 12

Are you hopeful about your future?

Year:

Year:

Year:

February 13

What is a tough life lesson you have had to learn?

Year: _____

Year: _____

Year: _____

February 14

Who do you want to be more like
or who do you look up to the most?

Year:

Year:

Year:

February 15

What is the worst emotional or
mental anguish you have endured?

Year: _____

_____

Year: _____

Year: _____

February 16

What do you like most about where we live?

Year: _____

Year: _____

Year: _____

February 17

What do you worry about?

Year: _____

Year: _____

Year: _____

February 18

What is something you screwed up and then tried to hide?

Year:

Year:

Year:

February 19

What is the scariest / creepiest
place you have ever been?

Year:

Year:

Year:

February 20

Do you think the world is improving
or getting worse? Why?

Year:

Year:

Year:

February 21

What's the biggest betrayal you have experienced?

Year: _____

Year: _____

Year: _____

February 22

What would be the greatest gift to receive?

Year: _____

Year: _____

Year: _____

February 23

What is something that you are dreading?

Year: _____

Year: _____

Year: _____

February 24

What makes you feel super fancy?

Year:

Year:

Year:

February 25

What would you want your obituary to say?

Year: _____

_____

_____

_____

Year: _____

_____

_____

_____

Year: _____

_____

_____

_____

February 26

What has taken up too much of your life?

Year: _____

Year: _____

Year: _____

February 27

What is the most heartening
realization you have come to?

Year: _____

_____

_____

_____

_____

_____

Year: _____

_____

_____

_____

_____

_____

Year: _____

_____

_____

_____

_____

_____

February 28

What was the most important
lesson you have had to learn?

Year:

Year:

Year:

February 29

What part of you still needs a lot of work?

Year: _____

_____

_____

_____

_____

Year: _____

_____

_____

_____

_____

Year: _____

_____

_____

_____

_____

March 1

What are some words of wisdom that have stuck with you all these years?

Year:

Year:

Year:

March 2

How well do you know yourself?

Year: _____

Year: _____

Year: _____

March 3

What is your best (not worst) flaw?

Year:

Year:

Year:

March 4

How forgiving are you?

Year: _____

_____

_____

_____

Year: _____

_____

_____

_____

Year: _____

_____

_____

_____

March 5

Are you ashamed of anything you did in the past?

Year:

Year:

Year:

March 6

Do you prefer living in the countryside,
in a town, or in a big city? Why?

Year: _____

Year: _____

Year: _____

March 7

What is your fondest memory from a vacation?

Year:

Year:

Year:

March 8

What are some of the most
pleasant sensations for you?

Year: _____

Year: _____

Year: _____

March 9

Are you happy with the career path you chose?

Year: _____

Year: _____

Year: _____

March 10

What is the most unethical thing you do regularly?

Year: _____

Year: _____

Year: _____

March 11

What job do you think you were born to do?

Year:

Year:

Year:

March 12

What's the biggest financial mistake you've made?

Year:

Year:

Year:

March 13

What was the most painful thing to hear?

Year:

Year:

Year:

March 14

What biases do you think you have?

Year: _____

Year: _____

Year: _____

March 15

What are you battling that you don't tell anyone about?

Year: _____

Year: _____

Year: _____

March 16

What luxury do you enjoy treating yourself to?

Year: _____

Year: _____

Year: _____

March 17

What do you most like to do
when you have alone time?

Year:

Year:

Year:

March 18

What do you want to be remembered for?

Year: _____

_____
_____
_____
_____
_____
_____

Year: _____

_____
_____
_____
_____
_____
_____
_____

Year: _____

_____
_____
_____
_____
_____
_____

March 19

Do you believe in good luck and bad luck?

Year:

Year:

Year:

March 20

What is something that a lot of people
are afraid of, but you are not?

Year: _____

_____

_____

_____

Year: _____

_____

_____

_____

Year: _____

_____

_____

_____

March 21

If you could open a business, what
type would you open?

Year:

Year:

Year:

March 22

What untrue thing did you believe
for an incredibly long time?

Year: _____

_____

_____

_____

_____

_____

_____

Year: _____

_____

_____

_____

_____

_____

_____

Year: _____

_____

_____

_____

_____

_____

_____

March 23

What were two important turning points in your life?

Year: _____

Year: _____

Year: _____

March 24

What animal are you most afraid of?

Year: _____

_____

_____

_____

_____

_____

Year: _____

_____

_____

_____

_____

_____

Year: _____

_____

_____

_____

_____

_____

March 25

What scandal happened in your area when you were growing up?

Year:

Year:

Year:

March 26

How well do you think you would handle prison?

Year: _____

Year: _____

Year: _____

March 27

What is the most awkward social situation you have been in?

Year: _____

_____
_____
_____
_____

Year: _____

_____
_____
_____
_____

Year: _____

_____
_____
_____
_____

March 28

What is something that scares you on a daily basis?

Year: _____

Year: _____

Year: _____

March 29

When was the last time you cried? Why?

Year: _____

Year: _____

Year: _____

March 30

What is the most peaceful night of sleep you have had?

Year: _____

_____
_____
_____
_____

Year: _____

_____
_____
_____
_____

Year: _____

_____
_____
_____
_____

March 31

What is the most dangerous thing you would consider doing?

Year: _____

Year: _____

Year: _____

April 1

What is your biggest regret?

Year: _____

Year: _____

Year: _____

April 2

Is it better to trust people or not? And why?

Year:

Year:

Year:

April 3

What do you think your best personality traits are?

Year: _____

_____

_____

_____

_____

_____

_____

Year: _____

_____

_____

_____

_____

_____

_____

Year: _____

_____

_____

_____

_____

_____

April 4

What do you take for granted?

Year: _____

Year: _____

Year: _____

April 5

What's the most stressful situation you have been in?

Year:

Year:

Year:

April 6

What's the most ambitious thing you've attempted?

Year:

Year:

Year:

April 7

How often do you change your
opinions on the world?

Year: _____

_____

_____

_____

_____

_____

Year: _____

_____

_____

_____

_____

_____

Year: _____

_____

_____

_____

_____

April 8

What's the biggest opportunity you were given?

Year: _____

Year: _____

Year: _____

April 9

What question do you wish people
would ask more often?

Year: _____

Year: _____

Year: _____

April 10

What are you most sentimental about?

Year:

Year:

Year:

April 11

Do you think more people look
down on you or up to you? Why?

Year: _____

Year: _____

Year: _____

April 12

What question do you most want an answer to?

Year:

Year:

Year:

April 13

What are some of the telltale signs of a shallow person?

Year: _____

_____

_____

_____

_____

Year: _____

_____

_____

_____

_____

Year: _____

_____

_____

_____

_____

April 14

What do you look forward to most in the day?

Year: _____

Year: _____

Year: _____

April 15

If you could instantly learn a talent or skill, what would you want to know how to do?

Year: _____

Year: _____

Year: _____

April 16

When is your favorite time of day, and why?

Year:

Year:

Year:

April 17

What are the best and worst things about life today?

Year: _____

Year: _____

Year: _____

April 18

What is the most rewarding thing
in your daily routine?

Year:

Year:

Year:

April 19

What weird thing stresses you out more than it should?

Year: _____

_____
_____
_____
_____

Year: _____

_____
_____
_____
_____

Year: _____

_____
_____
_____
_____

April 20

When do you feel you are really in your element?

Year:

Year:

Year:

April 21

How likely are you to believe in conspiracy theories?

Year:

Year:

Year:

April 22

What are some crazy stories of your younger days?

Year: _____

_____

_____

Year: _____

_____

_____

Year: _____

_____

_____

April 23

What is the best way for someone to improve themselves?

Year: _____

_____

_____

_____

_____

_____

_____

Year: _____

_____

_____

_____

_____

_____

_____

Year: _____

_____

_____

_____

_____

_____

_____

April 24

What was the most productive time in your life?

Year:

Year:

Year:

April 25

What three words best describe you?

Year: _____

_____

_____

_____

Year: _____

_____

_____

_____

Year: _____

_____

_____

_____

April 26

If you dropped everything and went on a road trip, where would you go, and why?

Year:

Year:

Year:

April 27

How well do you function under a lot of pressure?

Year: _____

Year: _____

Year: _____

April 28

What is your main weakness?

Year: _____

Year: _____

Year: _____

April 29

What are two of the most crucial events in your life?

Year: _____

Year: _____

Year: _____

April 30

What is the biggest favor you have done for someone?

Year:

Year:

Year:

May 1

How does your current morning routine
compare to your ideal morning routine?

Year: _____

_____

_____

_____

_____

_____

Year: _____

_____

_____

_____

_____

_____

Year: _____

_____

_____

_____

_____

_____

May 2

What are you purposefully ignoring even though
you know you should probably deal with it?

Year:

Year:

Year:

May 3

Is there anything you did wrong for years and years, only to discover later that you were doing it wrong?

Year: _____

_____

_____

_____

_____

_____

Year: _____

_____

_____

_____

_____

_____

Year: _____

_____

_____

_____

_____

_____

May 4

What brings you the most joy?

Year:

Year:

Year:

May 5

What do you wish you were better at?

Year: _____

_____

_____

_____

Year: _____

_____

_____

_____

Year: _____

_____

_____

_____

May 6

What is something your parents did or used to do that really embarrassed you?

Year: _____

Year: _____

Year: _____

May 7

What seemingly insignificant thing did someone say when you were a child that has stuck with you?

Year: _____

_____
_____
_____
_____
_____

Year: _____

_____
_____
_____
_____
_____

Year: _____

_____
_____
_____
_____
_____

May 8

What is the best or worst thing you inherited from your parents?

Year: _____

Year: _____

Year: _____

May 9

What made you realize that your parents were just human like everyone else?

Year: _____

_____

_____

_____

_____

_____

Year: _____

_____

_____

_____

_____

_____

Year: _____

_____

_____

_____

_____

_____

May 10

What habits do you still have from childhood?

Year:

Year:

Year:

May 11

What family vacations did you take as a child?

Year: _____

_____

Year: _____

_____

Year: _____

_____

May 12

How traditionally "normal" was your family?

Year:

Year:

Year:

May 13

How do you want to be different than your parents?

Year: _____

_____
_____
_____

_____
_____
_____

Year: _____

_____
_____
_____

_____
_____
_____

Year: _____

_____
_____
_____

_____
_____
_____

May 14

What school subjects did you like and hate most?

Year: _____

Year: _____

Year: _____

May 15

What unique game of pretend
did you play as a child?

Year: _____

_____
_____
_____
_____
_____

Year: _____

_____
_____
_____
_____
_____

Year: _____

_____
_____
_____
_____
_____

May 16

What movie scarred you as a child or as an adult?

Year:

Year:

Year:

May 17

What irrational fears did you have as a child?

Year: _____

_____

_____

_____

_____

_____

Year: _____

_____

_____

_____

_____

_____

Year: _____

_____

_____

_____

_____

May 18

What toys played a significant part in your childhood?

Year:

Year:

Year:

May 19

What are some of your earliest memories?

Year: _____

_____
_____
_____
_____
_____
_____

Year: _____

_____
_____
_____
_____
_____
_____

Year: _____

_____
_____
_____
_____
_____
_____

May 20

What is something I did that you thought was exceptionally kind or thoughtful?

Year: _____

Year: _____

Year: _____

May 21

What new hobbies or activities would you
like to try together as a couple?

Year: _____

Year: _____

Year: _____

May 22

What is our greatest strength as a couple?

Year:

Year:

Year:

May 23

What could we do to make our relationship stronger?

Year: _____

Year: _____

Year: _____

May 24

What is something small we
can do daily for each other?

Year:

Year:

Year:

May 25

How much alone time should we give each other?

Year: _____

Year: _____

Year: _____

May 26

What questions should partners ask before marriage?

Year:

Year:

Year:

May 27

What do I do that makes you the happiest?

Year:

Year:

Year:

May 28

How important is it for individuals in a relationship to maintain their own separate identity?

Year: _____

Year: _____

Year: _____

May 29

What makes our relationship better than others?

Year: _____

Year: _____

Year: _____

May 30

What do you think our life will
look like in 10 years?

Year: _____

Year: _____

Year: _____

May 31

What would bring us closer together as a couple?

Year: _____

Year: _____

Year: _____

June 1

What kind of memories do you want to make together?

Year: _____

Year: _____

Year: _____

June 2

What do you think the most essential thing
in a successful relationship is?

Year: _____

Year: _____

Year: _____

June 3

What is your favorite way we spend time together?

Year:

Year:

Year:

June 4

What is your favorite gift I have given you?

Year: _____

Year: _____

Year: _____

June 5

Where do you want to live when we retire?

Year: _____

_____

_____

_____

_____

_____

Year: _____

_____

_____

_____

_____

_____

Year: _____

_____

_____

_____

_____

_____

June 6

In what areas do you think our personalities complement each other?

Year: _____

_____
_____
_____
_____
_____
_____

Year: _____

_____
_____
_____
_____
_____
_____

Year: _____

_____
_____
_____
_____
_____
_____

June 7

How well do you think we communicate?

Year: _____

_____

_____

_____

Year: _____

_____

_____

_____

Year: _____

_____

_____

_____

June 8

What adventure would you like to go on with me?

Year: _____

_____

_____

_____

_____

Year: _____

_____

_____

_____

_____

Year: _____

_____

_____

_____

_____

June 9

What is the best relationship
advice you have received?

Year:

Year:

Year:

June 10

What are some things you really like about me?

Year: _____

Year: _____

Year: _____

June 11

What's the hardest thing about a relationship?

Year:

Year:

Year:

June 12

What can I do to most help us?

Year: _____

Year: _____

Year: _____

June 13

What do you see as your role in our relationship?

Year:

Year:

Year:

June 14

What would be a deal breaker for our relationship, something you could not forgive?

Year: _____

Year: _____

Year: _____

June 15

What do you think would be the best way
to strengthen our relationship?

Year:

Year:

Year:

June 16

What makes us different than other couples?

Year: _____

_____

_____

_____

_____

_____

_____

Year: _____

_____

_____

_____

_____

_____

_____

Year: _____

_____

_____

_____

_____

_____

June 17

What are some of your relationship goals?

Year:

Year:

Year:

June 18

How realistic do you think
couples in movies and TV are?

Year: _____

Year: _____

Year: _____

June 19

What does a happy relationship look like to you?

Year:

Year:

Year:

June 20

How well do you think our sex drives match up?

Year: _____

_____

_____

_____

_____

_____

Year: _____

_____

_____

_____

_____

_____

Year: _____

_____

_____

_____

_____

June 21

What are you into, but have not told me about?

Year: _____

Year: _____

Year: _____

June 22

When am I at my sexiest?

Year: _____

Year: _____

Year: _____

June 23

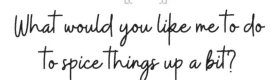

What would you like me to do to spice things up a bit?

Year:

Year:

Year:

June 24

What do I do outside the bedroom that turns you on?

Year: _____

Year: _____

Year: _____

June 25

Do you want to have children? How many?

Year:

Year:

Year:

June 26

What is the worst parenting mistake
a couple can make?

Year: _____

Year: _____

Year: _____

June 27

What is the best way to raise children?

Year:

Year:

Year:

June 28

How would we know if we did
our job as parents well?

Year: _____

Year: _____

Year: _____

June 29

Do you think it is more important for a couple with kids to focus on the kids more or each other? Why?

Year:

Year:

Year:

June 30

How do you think having kids will /
has changed our lives and relationship?

Year: _____

Year: _____

Year: _____

July 1

What would be the absolute perfect day?

Year: _____

Year: _____

Year: _____

July 2

What did you learn a little too late?

Year: _____

_____

_____

_____

_____

_____

Year: _____

_____

_____

_____

_____

_____

Year: _____

_____

_____

_____

_____

_____

July 3

What are you too hard on yourself for?

Year: _____

Year: _____

Year: _____

July 4

How often do you feel utterly worn down?

Year: _____

Year: _____

Year: _____

July 5

Who was the most giving person you have known?

Year:

Year:

Year:

July 6

What were the last two books that you read?

Year: _____

_____

_____

_____

Year: _____

_____

_____

_____

Year: _____

_____

_____

_____

July 7

What habits do you have that annoy other people?

Year: _____

Year: _____

Year: _____

July 8

What makes you nervous?

Year: _____

_____
_____
_____
_____
_____
_____

Year: _____

_____
_____
_____
_____
_____
_____

Year: _____

_____
_____
_____
_____
_____
_____

July 9

What makes you angrier than it should?

Year: _____

_____
_____
_____

Year: _____

_____
_____
_____

Year: _____

_____
_____
_____

July 10

What is the biggest lessons you have learned from previous relationships?

Year: _____

_____

_____

_____

_____

_____

_____

Year: _____

_____

_____

_____

_____

_____

_____

Year: _____

_____

_____

_____

_____

_____

July 11

What habit do you have that you
think not many other people have?

Year:

Year:

Year:

July 12

What do most people overestimate
or underestimate about you?

Year: _____

_____
_____
_____
_____
_____
_____

Year: _____

_____
_____
_____
_____
_____
_____

Year: _____

_____
_____
_____
_____
_____

July 13

What is something you probably should do, but will never do?

Year: _____

_____

_____

_____

_____

Year: _____

_____

_____

_____

_____

Year: _____

_____

_____

_____

_____

July 14

What do you most look forward to about getting older?

Year: _____

_____
_____
_____
_____
_____

Year: _____

_____
_____
_____
_____
_____

Year: _____

_____
_____
_____
_____
_____

July 15

What is the biggest sign of weakness in a person?

Year:

Year:

Year:

July 16

What is something you tried really hard to like but just could not?

Year: _____

Year: _____

Year: _____

July 17

What makes you different from most people?

Year:

Year:

Year:

July 18

What was the best mistake you have made?

Year: _____

_____

_____

_____

_____

Year: _____

_____

_____

_____

_____

Year: _____

_____

_____

_____

_____

July 19

How do you feel about pets and animals?

Year: _____

_____

_____

_____

_____

Year: _____

_____

_____

_____

_____

Year: _____

_____

_____

_____

_____

July 20

What silly thing do you take a lot of pride in?

Year: _____

_____

_____

_____

_____

_____

_____

Year: _____

_____

_____

_____

_____

_____

_____

Year: _____

_____

_____

_____

_____

_____

July 21

What unnecessary products or services
do you consider necessary?

Year:

Year:

Year:

July 22

What is the best conspiracy theory you can make up on the spot?

Year: _____

Year: _____

Year: _____

July 23

What do people really need to chill out about?

Year: _____

Year: _____

Year: _____

July 24

What scrambles your brain when you think about it?

Year: _____

Year: _____

Year: _____

July 25

What crazy things will you do if you become rich?

Year: _____

Year: _____

Year: _____

July 26

What is the last thing you Googled?

Year: _____

Year: _____

Year: _____

July 27

What is a lame joke you use on a regular basis?

Year:

Year:

Year:

July 28

If you could change your name, what would it be?

Year: _____

_____

_____

_____

Year: _____

_____

_____

_____

Year: _____

_____

_____

_____

July 29

What chore do you dread most?

Year:

Year:

Year:

July 30

What would you do first if you could fly?

Year: _____

_____

_____

_____

_____

Year: _____

_____

_____

_____

_____

Year: _____

_____

_____

_____

_____

July 31

If you had a secret lair, what would it be like?

Year:

Year:

Year:

August 1

What is your favorite waste of time?

Year: _____

_____
_____
_____
_____

Year: _____

_____
_____
_____
_____

Year: _____

_____
_____
_____
_____

August 2

What do you fear about the future?

Year:

Year:

Year:

August 3

What about yoursef scares you the most?

Year: _____

_____
_____
_____
_____

_____
_____
_____

Year: _____

_____
_____
_____

_____
_____
_____

Year: _____

_____
_____
_____
_____

_____
_____
_____

August 4

What is the worst dream you have had recently?

Year:

Year:

Year:

August 5

What do you get overly emotional about?

Year: _____

_____

Year: _____

_____

Year: _____

_____

August 6

What is the quickest way to make you angry?

Year:

Year:

Year:

August 7

What is on your bucket list?

Year: _____

_____
_____
_____
_____
_____
_____
_____
_____

Year: _____

_____
_____
_____
_____
_____
_____
_____
_____

Year: _____

_____
_____
_____
_____
_____
_____
_____
_____

August 8

What would you want your funeral to be like?

Year:

Year:

Year:

August 9

What quirks does your body have?

Year: _____

Year: _____

Year: _____

August 10

What brutally honest truth about yourself can you share with me?

Year:

Year:

Year:

August 11

What is it like to be you?

Year: _____

Year: _____

Year: _____

August 12

When did you try hard, and it wasn't enough?

Year:

Year:

Year:

August 13

What are you a snob about?

Year: _____

_____

_____

_____

_____

_____

Year: _____

_____

_____

_____

_____

_____

Year: _____

_____

_____

_____

_____

_____

August 14

What odd thing are you fascinated by?

Year: _____

Year: _____

Year: _____

August 15

What about your appearance would you change?

Year: _____

Year: _____

Year: _____

August 16

What is the most alone you have ever been?

Year:

Year:

Year:

August 17

What makes you feel alive?

Year: _____

_____

_____

_____

_____

Year: _____

_____

_____

_____

_____

Year: _____

_____

_____

_____

_____

August 18

In what situations do you act least like yourself?

Year: _____

Year: _____

Year: _____

August 19

What do you value most?

Year: _____

_____
_____
_____
_____
_____
_____
_____

Year: _____

_____
_____
_____
_____
_____
_____
_____

Year: _____

_____
_____
_____
_____
_____
_____
_____

August 20

What are you really obsessed about?

Year:

Year:

Year:

August 21

Who or what is holding you back in life?

Year: _____

_____

_____

_____

_____

Year: _____

_____

_____

_____

_____

Year: _____

_____

_____

_____

_____

August 22

What is the most painful text you have received?

Year:

Year:

Year:

August 23

What are some things you hid from your parents?

Year: _____

_____
_____
_____
_____

Year: _____

_____
_____
_____
_____

Year: _____

_____
_____
_____
_____

August 24

If you could go back and change just one decision
you made, what would you change?

Year:

Year:

Year:

August 25

What's the most memorable call you've taken or made?

Year: _____

_____

_____

_____

_____

_____

Year: _____

_____

_____

_____

_____

_____

Year: _____

_____

_____

_____

_____

_____

August 26

What movie title best describes your life so far?

Year: _____

_____

Year: _____

_____

Year: _____

_____

August 27

Who have you purposely cut out of your life? Why?

Year: _____

_____

_____

_____

_____

_____

Year: _____

_____

_____

_____

_____

_____

Year: _____

_____

_____

_____

_____

_____

August 28

Who is the nicest person you have ever met?

Year:

Year:

Year:

August 29

What is your most beautiful memory?

Year: _____

_____

_____

_____

Year: _____

_____

_____

_____

Year: _____

_____

_____

_____

August 30

How much have you changed in the past year?

Year:

Year:

Year:

August 31

What do you wish you had/hadn't said?

Year: _____

Year: _____

Year: _____

September 1

What is the riskiest thing you have ever done?

Year: _____

_____

_____

_____

Year: _____

_____

_____

_____

Year: _____

_____

_____

_____

September 2

When was the last time you were really,
really wrong about something?

Year: _____

_____

_____

_____

Year: _____

_____

_____

_____

Year: _____

_____

_____

_____

September 3

What is the most uncomfortable thing
you have had to tell someone?

Year:

Year:

Year:

September 4

How well do your family members get along?

Year: _____

Year: _____

Year: _____

September 5

Who is currently the black sheep in your family?

Year:

Year:

Year:

September 6

Who is the most difficult person
you must deal with? Why?

Year: _____

Year: _____

Year: _____

September 7

When did you think you knew someone, but they turned out to be an entirely different person?

Year:

Year:

Year:

September 8

What is your number one rule in a relationship?

Year: _____

Year: _____

Year: _____

September 9

Who in your life has the healthiest relationship?

Year:

Year:

Year:

September 10

What did you learn about relationships
from watching your mother and father?

Year: _____

Year: _____

Year: _____

September 11

What group of people do you find it
impossible to take seriously?

Year:

Year:

Year:

September 12

What makes you feel old?

Year: _____

_____
_____
_____
_____
_____
_____

Year: _____

_____
_____
_____
_____
_____
_____

Year: _____

_____
_____
_____
_____
_____
_____

September 13

What is considered normal but really shouldn't be?

Year:

Year:

Year:

September 14

What is the worst emotion?

Year: _____

Year: _____

Year: _____

September 15

What do people most often take for granted?

Year:

Year:

Year:

September 16

What is something that does not live up to the hype?

Year: _____

_____

Year: _____

_____

Year: _____

_____

September 17

What is the biggest waste of money?

Year:

Year:

Year:

September 18

What do you need advice about?

Year: _____

Year: _____

Year: _____

September 19

Who do you aspire to be more like, and why?

Year:

Year:

Year:

September 20

What do you find yourself often getting into arguments about?

Year:

_____

Year:

_____

Year:

_____

September 21

When in history was the best time to be alive?

Year: _____

Year: _____

Year: _____

September 22

What behavior makes you think someone has a lot of class?

Year: _____

Year: _____

Year: _____

September 23

What bad experience should everyone have to go through?

Year:

Year:

Year:

September 24

What do you wish you could stop doing?

Year: _____

_____
_____
_____
_____
_____

Year: _____

_____
_____
_____
_____
_____

Year: _____

_____
_____
_____
_____
_____

September 25

What social issue deserves more attention?

Year:

Year:

Year:

September 26

Where would your perfect place to settle down be?

Year: _____

_____

_____

_____

_____

Year: _____

_____

_____

_____

_____

Year: _____

_____

_____

_____

September 27

What movie changed how you looked at the world?

Year:

Year:

Year:

September 28

What is a song you cannot stand listening to?

Year: _____

_____
_____
_____
_____
_____
_____

Year: _____

_____
_____
_____
_____
_____
_____

Year: _____

_____
_____
_____
_____
_____
_____

September 29

Who would be the best fictional character to have as a best friend?

Year:

Year:

Year:

September 30

Have you ever cheated on someone before?
What happened?

Year: _____

Year: _____

Year: _____

October 1

What are the three most annoying
things a partner can do?

Year:

Year:

Year:

October 2

What three objects that you own do you value most?

Year: _____

Year: _____

Year: _____

October 3

What is your idea of a perfect Saturday night?

Year:

Year:

Year:

October 4

What do you think is worth spending extra on to get the best?

Year: _____

Year: _____

Year: _____

October 5

What do you know that you aren't supposed to know?

Year: _____

Year: _____

Year: _____

October 6

What is the most romantic thing you have heard
about someone doing for someone else?

Year: _____

_____

_____

_____

_____

_____

_____

Year: _____

_____

_____

_____

_____

_____

_____

Year: _____

_____

_____

_____

_____

_____

October 7

What do you need to vent about now?

Year: _____

Year: _____

Year: _____

October 8

What are some unwritten rules in your family?

Year: _____

Year: _____

Year: _____

October 9

What's a surprising thing you have learned recently?

Year:

Year:

Year:

October 10

What is your idea of succeeding?

Year: _____

_____

_____

_____

_____

Year: _____

_____

_____

_____

_____

Year: _____

_____

_____

_____

_____

October 11

What do you think about when you
are lying in bed unable to sleep?

Year:

Year:

Year:

October 12

What food do you crave most?

Year: _____

Year: _____

Year: _____

October 13

What is the best way to spend a rainy afternoon?

Year:

Year:

Year:

October 14

What are some things you feel compelled to do?

Year: _____

_____

_____

_____

_____

_____

_____

Year: _____

_____

_____

_____

_____

_____

_____

Year: _____

_____

_____

_____

_____

_____

_____

October 15

What slang or trend makes you feel old?

Year:

Year:

Year:

October 16

What is something that was way better
than you thought it would be?

Year: _____

Year: _____

Year: _____

October 17

What are some things you have seen that you wish you could unsee?

Year:

Year:

Year:

October 18

What book has had the biggest impact on you?

Year: _____

_____

_____

_____

_____

_____

Year: _____

_____

_____

_____

_____

_____

_____

Year: _____

_____

_____

_____

_____

_____

October 19

What would be the perfect pet? Why?

Year:

Year:

Year:

October 20

If you could ask one question about your future,
what would you ask?

Year: _____

_____

_____

_____

_____

_____

Year: _____

_____

_____

_____

_____

_____

Year: _____

_____

_____

_____

_____

October 21

What would your dream home look like?

Year:

Year:

Year:

October 22

What do you wish you had started a long time ago?

Year: _____

Year: _____

Year: _____

October 23

What do you find hilarious but most people do not find funny?

Year: _____

Year: _____

Year: _____

October 24

What has been the best of year of your life so far?

Year: _____

Year: _____

Year: _____

October 25

What is your favorite thing to do on the internet?

Year:

Year:

Year:

October 26

What do you spend way too much money on?

Year: _____

_____

_____

_____

Year: _____

_____

_____

_____

Year: _____

_____

_____

_____

October 27

What do you judge people for most often?

Year:

Year:

Year:

October 28

What is something you can do that most people can't?

Year: _____

_____

_____

_____

_____

_____

Year: _____

_____

_____

_____

_____

_____

Year: _____

_____

_____

_____

_____

October 29

How do you calm yourself down when you are angry?

Year:

Year:

Year:

October 30

What do you have a hard time with but most people find quite easy?

Year: _____

_____
_____
_____

_____
_____
_____

Year: _____

_____
_____
_____

_____
_____
_____

Year: _____

_____
_____
_____

_____
_____
_____

October 31

What is the most impressive skill you have?

Year:

Year:

Year:

November 1

Who is the most fascinating person you have met?

Year: _____

Year: _____

Year: _____

November 2

Are you a morning person or a night owl?

Year:

Year:

Year:

November 3

What music artist do you never get tired of? Why?

Year: _____

_____

_____

_____

_____

_____

Year: _____

_____

_____

_____

_____

_____

Year: _____

_____

_____

_____

_____

November 4

What is your favorite app on your phone? Why?

Year: _____

_____

_____

_____

_____

_____

Year: _____

_____

_____

_____

_____

_____

Year: _____

_____

_____

_____

_____

_____

November 5

Who are your kind of people?

Year: _____

_____

Year: _____

_____

Year: _____

_____

November 6

What is the silliest fear you have?

Year: _____

_____

_____

_____

_____

_____

Year: _____

_____

_____

_____

_____

_____

Year: _____

_____

_____

_____

_____

_____

November 7

If you could give everyone just one piece
of advice, what would it be?

Year: _____

_____
_____
_____
_____
_____
_____

Year: _____

_____
_____
_____
_____
_____

Year: _____

_____
_____
_____
_____
_____

November 8

What wrong assumptions do people make about you?

Year: _____

Year: _____

Year: _____

November 9

What is the dumbest thing you have ever done?

Year: _____

Year: _____

Year: _____

November 10

When do you feel most out of place?

Year: _____

Year: _____

Year: _____

November 11

What did you do last summer?

Year: _____

_____

_____

_____

_____

_____

_____

Year: _____

_____

_____

_____

_____

_____

_____

Year: _____

_____

_____

_____

_____

_____

_____

November 12

What are you most grateful for?

Year:

Year:

Year:

November 13

What is the most essential part of a friendship?

Year: _____

_____
_____
_____
_____
_____
_____

Year: _____

_____
_____
_____
_____
_____
_____

Year: _____

_____
_____
_____
_____
_____

November 14

What is the strangest phone conversation you've had?

Year:

Year:

Year:

November 15

Who is your favorite superhero, and why?

Year: _____

_____
_____
_____
_____
_____
_____

Year: _____

_____
_____
_____
_____
_____
_____

Year: _____

_____
_____
_____
_____
_____
_____

November 16

What do you like but are kind of
embarrassed to admit?

Year:

Year:

Year:

November 17

What is the best meal you have ever had?

Year: _____

_____
_____
_____
_____
_____

Year: _____

_____
_____
_____
_____
_____

Year: _____

_____
_____
_____
_____
_____

November 18

What is the worst advice someone has given you?

Year:

Year:

Year:

November 19

What are your top 3 favorite things to talk about?

Year: _____

Year: _____

Year: _____

November 20

What do you care least about?

Year:

Year:

Year:

November 21

What are people often surprised to learn about you?

Year: _____

Year: _____

Year: _____

November 22

What small things brighten up your day?

Year:

Year:

Year:

November 23

What do you miss about life 10 or 20 years ago?

Year: _____

_____
_____
_____
_____
_____

Year: _____

_____
_____
_____
_____
_____

Year: _____

_____
_____
_____
_____
_____

November 24

What is the last new thing you tried?

Year:

Year:

Year:

November 25

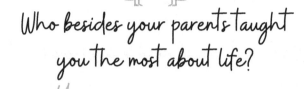

Who besides your parents taught you the most about life?

Year: _____

_____

_____

_____

Year: _____

_____

_____

_____

Year: _____

_____

_____

_____

November 26

What is the most spontaneous thing you've done?

Year:

Year:

Year:

November 27

How much social interaction is too much?

Year: _____

_____

_____

_____

_____

Year: _____

_____

_____

_____

_____

Year: _____

_____

_____

_____

_____

November 28

What are you looking forward to that's happening soon?

Year:

Year:

Year:

November 29

What is the worst or best job you have had?

Year: _____

Year: _____

Year: _____

November 30

What social situations do you try to avoid most?

Year:

Year:

Year:

December 1

What is the hardest you've worked for something?

Year: _____

Year: _____

Year: _____

December 2

What took you way too long to figure out?

Year:

Year:

Year:

December 3

What do you do differently than most people?

Year: _____

_____
_____
_____
_____

Year: _____

_____
_____
_____
_____

Year: _____

_____
_____
_____
_____

December 4

What do you hope never changes?

Year: _____

Year: _____

Year: _____

December 5

What are you absolutely determined to do?

Year: _____

_____

_____

_____

Year: _____

_____

_____

_____

Year: _____

_____

_____

_____

December 6

What do you wish you knew more about?

Year:

Year:

Year:

December 7

How different was your life one year ago?

Year: _____

_____
_____
_____

Year: _____

_____
_____
_____

Year: _____

_____
_____
_____

December 8

What fad or trend do you hope comes back?

Year:

Year:

Year:

December 9

What do you consider to be your best find?

Year: _____

Year: _____

Year: _____

December 10

What have you only recently formed an opinion on?

Year:

Year:

Year:

December 11

What is an ideal weekend for you?

Year: _____

Year: _____

Year: _____

December 12

Have you ever had your heart broken?

Year:

Year:

Year:

December 13

How do you honestly feel about monogamy?

Year: _____

_____
_____
_____
_____
_____

Year: _____

_____
_____
_____
_____
_____

Year: _____

_____
_____
_____
_____

December 14

In what circumstances do you think it's okay to fib?

Year:

Year:

Year:

December 15

What are you most passionate about in life?

Year: _____

Year: _____

Year: _____

December 16

Would you be willing to relocate for either of our jobs?

Year:

Year:

Year:

December 17

What keeps you going day to day?

Year: _____

_____

_____

_____

_____

Year: _____

_____

_____

_____

_____

Year: _____

_____

_____

_____

_____

December 18

Do you believe in reincarnation, or an afterlife?

Year:

Year:

Year:

December 19

How do you feel about adoption?

Year: _____

_____

_____

_____

_____

_____

Year: _____

_____

_____

_____

_____

_____

Year: _____

_____

_____

_____

_____

_____

December 20

Would you ever stay home to parent full-time?

Year:

Year:

Year:

December 21

What is the trait you value most?

Year: _____

_____
_____
_____
_____
_____
_____
_____
_____

Year: _____

_____
_____
_____
_____
_____
_____
_____
_____

Year: _____

_____
_____
_____
_____
_____
_____
_____
_____

December 22

What do you consider your greatest weakness?

Year:

Year:

Year:

December 23

Do you consider yourself a good friend? Why?

Year: _____

_____
_____
_____
_____
_____
_____

Year: _____

_____
_____
_____
_____
_____
_____

Year: _____

_____
_____
_____
_____
_____
_____

December 24

What does love look like to you?

Year:

Year:

Year:

December 25

What is the greatest accomplishment of your life?

Year: _____

Year: _____

Year: _____

December 26

What is your most treasured memory?

Year:

Year:

Year:

December 27

How do you feel about your relationship
with your mother?

Year: _____

Year: _____

Year: _____

December 28

When did you last talk to a stranger?

Year:

Year:

Year:

December 29

If you could trade lives with someone, who would it be?

Year: _____

_____

_____

_____

_____

Year: _____

_____

_____

_____

_____

Year: _____

_____

_____

_____

_____

December 30

What do you see yourself doing after retirement?

Year: _____

_____

_____

_____

_____

Year: _____

_____

_____

_____

_____

Year: _____

_____

_____

_____

_____

December 31

How much do you love me?

Year: _____

_____

_____

_____

Year: _____

_____

_____

_____

Year: _____

_____

_____

_____

Made in the USA
Las Vegas, NV
22 December 2023

83465249R00203